Dear Moses...

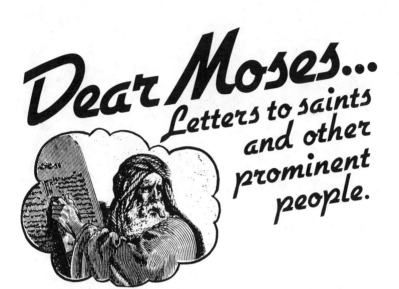

Dear Moses...
Letters to saints and other prominent people.

FROM LOIS DONAHUE
with illustrations by
R. AHLE

Our Sunday Visitor Inc.
200 Noll Plaza, Huntington, IN 46750

Library of Congress Catalogue No: 84-60743
ISBN 0-87973-699-2

Printed in the United States of America

DEDICATION

*To a loving God who
created so many caring,
patient, supportive people
and put them in my world.*

CONTENTS

EPIGRAPH

God breathed and there was life.
   He willed — there was hereafter.
God touched and there was love.
   God winked and there was laughter.

PREFACE

Dear Reader:

I know that people don't ordinarily share their personal letters with the world. To be honest, I feel a bit strange about it myself; but, you see, I still haven't worked my way up to ordinary. I'm the kind of "un-ordinary" person who has hot dogs and onion rings for breakfast, walks down UP escalators and is afflicted with chronic thought-wrinkle.

I assure you, however, that I am well-meaning, harmless and deeply in love with a Church which teaches compassionate tolerance toward those of us who are "different."

Speaking of church, I want you to be assured that I tried to go through official ecclesiastical channels before publication. I went to my priest, shook his hand, gave him my letters and asked procedure for obtaining an *imprimatur*. He read my letters, patted my hand and said he would pray for me. (Since that meeting, I have left the following instructions with the children: If the pastor calls, tell him we might move. If the bishop calls, apologize. If the pope calls, start a novena.)

You should also know that my husband reviewed

the book and said that it would never sell. BUT PLEASE NOTE! He said the same thing about stock in a new company planning to manufacture a synthetic fuel. (Their formula calls for the use of uneaten vegetable scraps from the plates of children and the remains of experimental casseroles scraped from the plates of husbands.)

HE WAS WRONG. The stock did sell. I bought both shares myself with my coupon-refund money, and as soon as he's out there getting 150 miles per gallon from Pollution-Free Vegelene, I'm going to tell him.

So, dear reader, welcome to my world — where, in fear and trembling, dwells my prayerful intention never to offend.

> With heart in mouth
> and tongue in cheek,
>
> *Lois*

I. OLD TESTAMENT

(Matriarchs, Prophets and Rulers)

Sarah, *Mrs. Abraham*
Senior Citizens' Division
Genesis, O.T.
18:9-15

Dear Sarah:

Up front, let me say that I don't blame you one bit for laughing. You must have thought those strangers were crazy, telling Abraham that you'd be pregnant within the year. You! — at *ninety*?

Now I'm sure that your consulting member of the Hebron Medical Association had told you No — that every woman who was a card-carrying member of Midwives Local No. 77 had told you No — and it's a cinch that any bookie in camp would have given top odds against it. With input opinions like that, no wonder you laughed; until, of course, that first siege of morning sickness.

And that's why I turn to you, Sarah. HOW DO WE KNOW WHOM TO BELIEVE? Today theologians disagree with the pope. Bishops disagree with the theologians. Priests disagree with bishops, and the pew people are taking potluck. It certainly raises questions in the minds of vintage CCD teachers like myself.

Oh, it isn't that I don't have faith, Sarah. If a burning bush walked up to me today and said that women were going to be ordained, I'd be the first one designing chasubles with bust measurements — but then, a burning bush that talks comes pretty plainly marked with the Supernatural Seal of Approval. However, as you found out, message bearers don't necessarily come winged, haloed or obviously miraculous — they just come, and then it's like taking the butter/margarine test.

Honestly, Sarah, every time I encounter someone with a strong vocal point of view, I wonder. For instance. . . .

This year I'm stuck with an eight-year-old space genius who knows more about interplanetary exploration than I know about the workings of my liver. He not only KNOWS that there are folks out there, but he's well-versed in their theology and comes on like a major prophet.

I've handled primary packaged imagination for years, but this kid intimidates me. He makes me feel like the Baltimore Catechism on Hans Küng's bookshelf. It's as if he knew that my first teaching certificate was issued before left-handed scissors and he's convinced that my progress has been minimal. His outer space is truly invading my inner peace.

Like the day I told the children the story of baby Moses in his basket in the river. Up went the boy's hand and he mesmerized the class with Quadran, who was set adrift in one of Jupiter's magnetic fields. When we talked about St. Paul and the flash of light from heaven, he countered with St. Zorf's conversion experience with cosmic rays.

Nobody reassures me. Nobody says, "Forget it, Teach — he's strictly from Fantasy Planet."

I dreamed last night that my little UFO pupil, Freddie, walked into class followed by a friend from the lower east side of Planet X. I gazed at a metallic spheroid with antenna ears, flashing eye-circles and egg-beater hands clutching a round Bible. He floated silently across the room and hovered at my kneecaps while his computer-panel chest lit up to read: "YOU ARE SCHEDULED TO UPDATE YOUR TEACHING CERTIFICATE ON MARS! A SPACE SHIP WILL PICK YOU UP SOMETIME NEXT SUMMER!"

I keep telling myself it was just a dream — nothing at all like *your* strangers. But, Sarah, just in case any-one from Heavenly Communications checks out an aluminum spheroid suit, will you give me a buzz? I'd like to pack a few things.

Confused and questioning,

16

Moses, *Plague Department Head*
Desert Travel Agency
Exodus, O.T.

9:13-35

Dear Moses:

Undoubtedly you and Aaron are no longer in charge of plagues, so I would appreciate your telling the new Plague Department head that he's not playing fair. With you it was one plague *after* another — hail *after* boils — but with him it's two at a time. The Church today is being plagued by words AND paper.

Just to give you an idea — at our interparish women's meeting, it took the president ten minutes to direct us to the restrooms. (Imagine how many crisp Christians we'd have had if she were in charge of emergency fire evacuation!)

And it isn't just the women. Recently I attended a workshop to hear a man speak on religious education. That's exactly what he did — spoke on . . . and on . . . and on . . . and on. Enough words came out of that man's mouth to cover his subject, fill eight columns of *Newsweek*, compose a lyrical ballad and still have plenty of letters left over for a good game of Scrabble.

While he was lulling me into nonproductive apathy, I dreamed that indulgence abuse was back — that every microphoned podium carried with it a guarantee of 300 days less time in purgatory for every 1,500 words.

17

I was jarred back to reality when someone handed me two mimeographed copies of the gentleman's verbal marathon. (In case I wanted to share my experience with friends.) Which brings me to the other half of this piggyback plague — PAPER.

It is literally impossible to attend a meeting today without risking a hernia carrying home the 8½-by-11-inch sheets distributed. Mr. Glad would certainly make a fortune if he showed up at every "instructive" gathering with extra-hefty tote bags.

To prove my point — following our last parish meeting, I came home with the following:

- A liturgical sheet complete with music, lyrics and guitar chords for those who wanted to strum along;

- Four pages of inspirational poetry for those of us who are slow responders to the call for spontaneous prayer;

- A get-acquainted questionnaire asking: at what age was I potty-trained? — how, as a Christian, could I relate to peanut-butter-and-jelly sandwiches? — what was my gut reaction to polka-dot vestments? — and had I ever tried to walk on water?

- A printed agenda (How could I possibly distinguish between the Pledge of Allegiance and the treasurer's report without a printed agenda?);

• A map of the hall so I could find the refreshment table;

• A detailed outline of how to conduct a neighborhood ecumenical garage sale;

• A projected 1999 calendar listing dates and departure times for anticipated retreats on the moon.

(The other 48 pages were excerpts from the four-volume contemporary best-seller *What Every Catholic Should Know About Beeswax Candles and Their Social Impact on the Families of Icelandic Bee Keepers.*)

Truly, Moses, it's getting almost unbearable, and I was wondering: Is this a "let-my-people-go" plague? If so, please send along the message that every family-sized pharaoh I know is willing to negotiate.

If it's merely a "you-got-yourself-into-it, now-get-yourself-out-of-it" plague, I'll look upon last night's *non-sanctioned* meeting as a glimmer of hope. It was held after dark in the crate-sized storage area behind the organ pipes above the choir loft. The atmosphere was friendly, the format informal, the goals realistic and the plan of action practical. We were out in an hour and, would you believe, the only paper circulated was a signature sheet petitioning our bishops to resist the pressure to declare the Xerox Corporation headquarters a national shrine.

With hope but seeking help,

Lois

P.S. Do you realize that two years ago I could have written my complaint in less than two paragraphs and would have sent you only one copy? Spooky isn't it?

Naomi, *Widow in Charge*
In-Law Appreciation Society
Ruth, O.T.

1-2-3-4

Dear Naomi:

I'm writing as one mother-in-law to another — with a question. How do you "tactfully" pass along to Ruth some of the things you must certainly have learned during the famine — things like food stretching with fish-dish helper or how to palatably disguise olive-pit wine?

The reason I ask is that our son and his wife are trying to furnish their small house in this time of eat-only inflation and I would like to share with them some helpful hints I picked up during the endless years when our decorating dollars either defected to the orthodontist or trickled through the life-support system which kept a Ford station wagon functioning long after even a used-car salesman would have pronounced it clinically dead.

I thought maybe I could disguise-print the following, address it to "occupant" and drop it into their mailbox after dark. See what you think.

DECORATORS ANONYMOUS TO THE RESCUE

First, be realistic. You will no doubt be utilizing a combination of garage-sale or rummage-sale purchases, sympathetic giveaways, trading-stamp premiums and NERVE. Working under the handicap of the first three, it is essential that you cultivate an abundance of the fourth. *Get gutsy*!

Become the nonconformist, the free spirit. If necessary, become the weird eccentric. But start slowly — like tinker-toy centerpieces and stacked-Tupperware lamp tables. Before you know it, you'll be able to set a Woolworth's Tiffany-glass lamp base with a ruffled shade on a driftwood end table with hardly a trace of nausea.

Next, convince yourself that you must accept compromise. Be willing to swap white shag for your sanity and pastel velvet for your children's emotional stability.

Also, you must realize that furniture abuse by children is epidemic and that no manufacturer has yet come up with a product able to withstand it. Plastic breaks, wood splits, foam rubber crumbles and even "Scotch" can only "gard" against a reasonably aggressive enemy.

All-metal furniture would seem to be the answer, but it, too, has shortcomings — the "short" might show up in your electrical wiring, and a passive occasional chair could suddenly become an instrument of capital punishment.

Stone carved furniture (à la Fred Flintstone) may offer durability, but you'll find yourself converting it

into driveway gravel when you discover that stone is cold, damp, hard and rough — unquestionably detrimental to hose, snag polyster, rheumatic conditions and unupholstered posteriors. Toss pillows don't even help. (Let me insert here that in a house with growing boys, *"toss"* pillow is a misnomer — "throw," "fling," "heave" or "pitch," maybe, but "toss" is reserved for bread slices, cookies, doughnuts and apples.)

Drapes of woven or braided crabgrass present a kind of back-to-nature environmentalist effect without necessarily conveying the fact that they stem both from economy and grow-your-own convenience.

In carpeting, you might consider choosing a play-dough color blend with coke, beer and milk highlights. While it is a definitive stain-blender, I must caution that it is also an object-concealer. Middle-aged eyesight cannot easily spot a two-inch Mustang or a runaway marble.

Furnishing a boy's room presents no problem if you ask yourself the simple question: "Boys' rooms are primarily used for what?" Answer: "Fighting — jumping — wrestling!" Therefore, why not go with wall-to-wall mattresses?

Need bedspreads for your daughters' beds? Simply sew together outgrown blouses, skirts, dresses and underwear. (You'll find them on the floor in the back of the closet.) Furniture pieces are of little consequence since they are seldom visible beneath the progression of dolls, records, posters, batons, stuffed animals, etc.

Don't let the cost of colored appliances stop you from updating your kitchen. Two pre-schoolers with felt pens can color a 36-inch stove in little less than an hour.

On kitchen and bathroom floors, why not lay nine-inch squares of compressed newspaper with bubble-gum flecks. They are highly absorbent and easily replaced.

Our next decorating flyer will explore the combination of two interesting concepts:

1. Storing food for the lean years ahead in easily handled, uniform-sized boxes.

2. Designing economical, functional and decorative furniture from easily handled, uniform-sized boxes.

Well, Naomi, do you think it's too obviously me? Will they guess who's sticking her nose in? There's only one giveaway I can think of. Our son might remember the year I made him use his Santa Claus felt pens to touch up the refrigerator.

Economically,

Lois

Moses *(follow-up)*

Dear Moses:

I just spent ten minutes in conversation with our youngest, convincing him that *he* was the one I wanted to cut the lawn. It reminded me of your conversation with the Lord when you tried your best to get out of the whole Exodus thing; and that, in turn, made me stop and think that there were probably a great many other very human conversations that were never recorded in the Bible.

For instance, I can imagine —

The older brother saying to the Prodigal Son, "Dad always liked you best."

Or a stranger, to the daybreak-to-evening vineyard worker: "How do you do, sir. I'm a union organizer."

Or an angry biblical mother to her son: "What's with the two baskets of bread crumbs? I sent you to the store for five barley loaves and two fish!"

Or Mary's parents: "What do you mean, Joseph isn't the father?"

Or the first person to encounter Jonah in Nineveh: "I don't care where you've been; go take a bath, you smell like fish!"

Or Lazarus to his sisters: "It's only been four days and already you've given away all my clothes?"

Good feeling to remember that those folks were human too. Makes me feel I've got a chance.

With hope,

Lois

Solomon, *King*
The Good Life Conglomerate
Proverbs, O.T.

12:27

Dear Solomon:

I've noticed, as I get older and realize how much closer I am to judgment, that my conscience keeps bringing up a lot of things that I'd crossed off my guilt list a long time ago.

Like four years ago, during my driver's license renewal test, when I copied two answers from the man standing next to me. I told my conscience at the time that no government licensing agency had the right to expect a woman on the tottering side of middle age, with bifocals, poor hearing and carrying around enough extra weight to make riding any two-wheeled vehicle look obscene, to know *anything* about motorcycle law.

But that's the way my conscience has been lately — picky, picky, picky.

As of last Tuesday, it's really been bugging me about something you brought up in your contribution to the Book of Proverbs. Namely, of all things — SLOTH.

It all started, as I said, last Tuesday. I was searching the house for a burglar-safe spot to hide a nine-inch plastic statue of Venus de Milo with a DISARM banner

29

across her chest, which I'm convinced will someday be a collector's item.

With my machete broom handle, I was chopping my way through the baseball mitt-underwear-album cover-dirty sock underbrush in our 15-year-old son's room when I spotted, half hidden by two hocky sticks and a broken ski, a small two-drawer chest. Almost instantly I recognized it.

Now I know that both my son and I have packrat tendencies and are definitely inclined to "stuff" rather than "straighten." Therefore, I was certain that the contents of both drawers had remained untouched for at least the past two years and would probably stay that way until either the fire department started making door-to-door inspections or we sold the house.

What a great spot to hide today's 89¢ plastic tossaway until it could become tomorrow's priceless sought-after. Carefully I tugged at the bottom drawer. It didn't budge — which told me its contents were packed in so tight that they had already solidified into one twelve-by-eight-by-six-inch block.

I took hold of the alphabet picture-block knobs on the top drawer. (I'd planned to change those ever since we'd replaced his nursery wallpaper.) Gently I pulled. Off came the front drawer panel and a waterfall of crumpled school papers fell to the floor. In such emergencies my immediate reaction is to do something procrastinatingly effective — like dropping a beanbag chair over the whole mess. Which I did. And it worked. Covered everything except for a half-page of paper on which were printed, neatly but boldly, three words. I glanced down at "SLOTH MEANS LAZY" as casually as if it had been a three-word ad for training bras and went off to the kitchen for my hourly snack break.

By the time I reached the cookie jar, my conscience had already shaped those three words into a pitchfork. I was not only thinking SLOTH but I was being pricked into thinking SEVEN CAPITAL SINS.

Now, truthfully, when I studied those "big seven" sins back in elementary school they all seemed to be just words. Words about as applicable to me as psoriasis, Geritol or canonization.

To begin with there was PRIDE. When you're a 13-year-old girl, taller than any boy in class, at least 15 pounds overweight, have braces on your teeth, pimples on your face and are struggling to maintain a C average, PRIDE just isn't a problem.

I remember lumping COVETOUNESS and LUST into the giggle category with adultery. I'm sure the more sophisticated girls in class knew what they were giggling about. The rest of us just giggled. You can't sin what you don't know — right?

ANGER — anger was for the extrovert, the strong, the assertive. With my beige personality, my tendency to be cowardly passive and having cultivated a fairly high tolerance level toward just about everything (thanks to imaginative escapism and homemade cookies), ANGER was certainly not a "now" concern.

GLUTTONY was definitely "somebody else's" sin. Gluttony was the fat lady in the circus freak show or grotesque Mr. Waddle, who took up half a pew in church. Even a plump teenager with high caloric cravings wouldn't consider GLUTTONY a part of her world.

ENVY — well, envy didn't apply to me either. If I'd have zeroed in my "wish-I-was" on the prettiest, smartest, most popular girl in class, that might have been ENVY. But to wish that I had whatever Elsie Klans had because Billy Petcher never threw dirt clods at Elsie Klans could certainly have been labeled "pathetic" but never ENVIOUS.

Now SLOTH in my grade school years, as in my son's, was defined as laziness. Well, with parents who issued weekly chore lists longer than the help-wanted columns in the Sunday edition of our local newspaper and who accepted no "can't do" excuse short of a full-body cast, I knew that SLOTH could certainly be scratched from this kid's examination of conscience.

So much for remembering — and so much for SLOTH — I thought, as I dragged myself back into the present. But it wasn't that simple. My conscience had done its work well. All day I kept thinking about the incident — seeing the word LAZY and feeling as guilty as the wife in a ring-around-the-collar commercial. (Most likely because just before my safari through Equatorial Back Bedroom I had spent an hour and a half doing nothing more than flipping through 28 back issues of *House Gorgeous* while all that time mildew was spreading in my shower, scalloped-potato scorch was drying up in my two-quart casserole and cobwebs were being spun in half the ceiling corners of my house.)

What I had rationalized as *relaxing* became lazy — became sloth — became sin. All because of some stupid piece of paper and an over-zealous, nit-picking conscience which seemed compelled to meet a sin-quota and resented the fact that I'd diminished its options by aging.

So, O Wise One of the Old Testament, I need to clear up a few things:

O.K., so I admit that on the spiritual side of things I'm a bit ho-hum. I know I slipped out of meatless Fridays as effortlessly as a fried egg out of a Teflon pan. I was so overjoyed when the Church lifted the midnight Communion fast that for a whole year I took 3 A.M. snacks to bed every Saturday night to celebrate — but will you please tell my conscience that being spiritually short on sacrifice and long on selfish is weakness, not sloth?

And I don't suppose it ever occurred to "Mr. Scrupulous" that there could be such a thing as heredi-tary laziness. I could very well be a descendant of some kickback, do-nothing-but-smell-pretty, look-pret-ty, dress-pretty and order-the-servants-around slothful Queen. I'll bet *lazy genes* never cross his mind.

33

Sounds as if I'm looking for excuses, doesn't it? Well, maybe I am, but more than that I'm looking for someone who understands.

Don't get me wrong, Solomon, what with a kingdom to run and a temple to build (to say nothing of the time and effort that must have gone into handling your "700 wives and 300 concubines"), I wouldn't expect you to understand "lazy" from personal experience any more than I'd expect honey-and-locust John the Baptist to understand gluttony! It did occur to me, however, since there was all that talk about lavish living, incense burning and forced labor, that you might just have a pretty good understanding of how to deal with conscience.

I sure could use some help.

Defensively,

Lois

Amos, *Prophet*
Repent and Reform Division
Amos, O.T.

1 — 9

Dear Amos:

You prophets have been my identifying hero figures ever since I tossed away my rose-colored glasses
and began to "see it like it is." From that moment on I
accepted life as a series of good news-bad news jokes
and felt morally obliged to warn others who had not
yet acquired that both-sides-of-the-coin vision. That's
why I come to you with such guilt feelings.

It all began way back when my nun friends first
started flipping through fashion magazines and talking
change. Ordinarily the warning signals would have
flashed within me. I would have seen far beyond
hemlines and hairstyles to corns, calluses, blow-dry
frizzies and blood-letting by razor. But no, I let my vision blur as I rejoiced with them over the prospect of
doing away with the torture-tight headpieces and lay-
ered wool with peek-a-boo flesh.

I'm sure I would have stumbled along blindly toward the fashion limbo somewhere between rigid and
ridiculous if I hadn't bumped into Sister Way-Out. Her
T-shirt, jeans and ankle straps threw me into shock.
By the time my vision cleared, it was too late. Pan-
dora's box had disintegrated, and we all stood blended

together like the annual meeting of Pantyhouse Anonymous. I could have cried.

Why hadn't I warned them that we pay the price for everything — that above every high heel is most likely a suffering spine, that around every dangling earring could very well be a throbbing lobe? Why hadn't I told them about polyester perspiration or the color-me-anything campaign against gray?

I hang my head in shame. Not one word had I spoken about the sadist who reshaped the hairshirt, shaved it, marketed it in mid-August and called it a girdle. No, the voice that had screamed hysterical warnings about crippling knee injuries to a twelve-year-old would-be linebacker was cowardly mute.

Why once, just once, couldn't I have extolled the blessings of "long?" Possibly, they didn't know that "long" is to spindle legs, knock-knees, varicose veins, thick ankles, runs, snags and wrinkled nylons what dark glasses are to bloodshot.

Perhaps they had never been told that what's thin at thirty might well be fat at forty, and that what might still be firm at forty sags for sure at sixty, and that "long from the shoulder" covers all that.

Oh, I've suffered for my silence. It's like a stab wound to my conscience each morning that I see Sister Used-to-Smile on the playground. The dark circles and the A.M. crankies tell me that she had to sleep on curlers again.

36

The day they called the ambulance for Sister Straight-and-Stringy I ran to the church and hid. I should have told her that asthma couldn't possibly win the battle against home-perm solution.

So I have lived with my guilt year after year — ever searching for ways to make amends to these dear sisters.

That's why, when I saw the TV commercial hinting that stockings with seams might be making a comeback, a thought occurred to me — and I'm asking:

Do you think it would clear my record at all if I wrote, as the voice of experience, to every short-skirted, bow-legged nun and warned her that seams would make her look like a walking parenthesis?

Or would that be just too little too late?

Repentantly,

Lois

II. NEW TESTAMENT

(Friends and Followers of the Lord)

Joseph, *Foster Parent*
Nazareth Carpenters' Assn.
Luke, N.T.

1:27

Dear St. Joseph:

I'm sure you never had the problem of talking too much. In fact, probably one of the reasons that you have always been on the top ten of my list of favorite saints is that you never said anything.

Oh, I don't mean you never said *anything.* I'm sure you said all the right things at the right time even if we never heard about it. But I just can't imagine you standing up at a meeting of the Independent Carpenters' Association and telling your fellow tradesmen that they had better quit hacking away at the local sycamore trees or they would have a pack of environmentalists on their backs — or, at the Yahweh Men's Society meeting to plan their annual Passover breakfast, I know you wouldn't have suggested that, for a change, they select a younger man for the main speaker — like your Son, for instance — assuring them that He would certainly present some fresh and innovative ideas.

No, that doesn't seem to be you — but, unfortunately, it's me.

For example, at last night's parish meeting I stood up and gave my unsolicited, off-the-top-of-my-head,

1947-mentality reaction to the otherwise unanimous decision to consider the introduction of contemporary music into the liturgy. The fact that I'm about as much an authority on liturgical music as our 15-year-old is on denture creams didn't cross my mind until our choir director gave me one of those "message" looks that one sees so often during hotly contested divorce cases. Instantly I knew I'd done it again.

But did that teach me a lesson? Of course not. Later I asked point blank: "Is it true that some ninny suggested having someone in a bunny costume hop up the aisle with the Offertory gifts during the children's Easter Mass?" Now *you* would either have avoided raising the question at all or at least rephrased it so as not to have had the embarrassment of facing Sister Mary Louise (the favorite teacher in our elementary school) when she identified herself as "the ninny." I know that anyone like yourself, who was apparently as comfortable with a cave full of shepherds as with three Eastern V.I.P.'s, would have been more diplomatic. I'm about as subtle as roach killer.

Let's face it. I know. You know. Everybody knows. *People like you better if you just listen!*

I write it with toothpaste on the bathroom mirror when I'm getting ready to go out. I trace it in the dust on the car hood before I pull out of the driveway. I visualize it in large red graffiti letters on the outside of any door I'm about to enter. But I step inside the room and zap! The mere sight of a gathering flips my "on" switch. From that moment you can safely bet that sooner or later I'll give my opinion, offer advice or ask a question that will put me on the eligible list to receive a boo-boo bumper sticker from Toastmasters International reading: "IF YOU HAVE TWO LEFT FEET — TRY PUTTING THEM BOTH IN YOUR MOUTH AT ONCE!" I could just die.

Would you believe that once I even told our pastor that whoever was responsible for the Easter Alleluia banner hanging from floor to ceiling in our church sanctuary was either anatomically blind or hung-up on kindergarten stick figures with 28-inch torsos and 62-inch arms? And I didn't have sense enough to stop there: I suggested that he try to peddle it at some church-goods swap meet for a few bucks and buy an imprimatur stamp for our parish library.

It happens everyplace I go. Even after baby showers or Tupperware parties or microwave cooking demonstrations I lie awake for hours reciting my Litany of Shouldn't-Have-Saids.

And it seems to be getting progressively worse. At first I needed group turn-on. No more. Now it's one on one — bank tellers, crossing guards, meter readers, benchwarmers. Age, size, sex, state of consciousness, religious or political affiliation raise no barriers for me. Were I multilingual, I'm sure I'd branch out even farther.

Oh, Joseph, it's agonizing. Meetings are being scheduled and I'm not notified; groups disintegrate when someone sees me coming; invitations arrive the day *after* the party. In irrational moments I want to tear out my tongue and donate it to perpetual-motion research. And it appears hopeless. My affliction seems to be neither temporary nor terminal: like dust on my venetian blinds, it's just *always there*.

You don't know how many conscience floggings I've imposed upon myself trying to decide its cause. Right now, egotistical pride and ignorant insecurity are running neck and neck for first place. It hasn't been easy eliminating less ego-destructive reasons that have crossed my mind.

Once I even considered the possibility that I had been given the gift of tongues and, because of some devilish intervention, my gift-tongue proved to be functionally defective.

My husband hasn't been much help. He suggested either having my jaws wired or my vocal chords tied. Needless to say, Joseph, I'm looking for alternative options. If you have any, please get in touch. If not, thanks anyway for listening. I just had to talk.

Incessantly,

Lois

Peter, *Pope 1st*
Main Pearly Gate
Matthew, N.T.

16:17-19

Dear St. Peter:

I write to you begging help for my beloved, middle-aged husband. He's still suffering through the change (liturgical change, that is) and I'm worried. Since you had a bit of a struggle with the circumcision transition, I feel you can "relate."

He's a good man, Peter — with Irish roots that are post-Reformation and pre-Vatican II. He was weaned on a Rosary pacifier, learned his nursery rhymes in Latin and breathed incense through his room humidifier.

But it's just been too much too fast. When they turned the altar around and removed the communion rail, he began to lock himself in the bathroom for ten minutes every Sunday morning and hum *Tantum Ergo*.

When 50-year-old Sister Martha, with her red shoes, pierced ears and Clairol rinse, shared our pew, his face turned scarlet and his knuckles turned white.

In truth, Peter, you're not the first I considered asking for help. I thought about our family physician but decided that not even this good, caring Orthodox

Jew could fully understand why an empty choir loft and a front pew filled with guitars, bagpipes, bongo drums, cowbells and musical saws would make a grown man cry.

I even tried calling the Free Spirit Clinic, staffed by theologically independent psychoanalysts, but when they said group therapy sessions were held between 1 and 5 A.M. each Saturday and that my husband was to bring with him a bag of confetti and a king-sized sheet, my woman's intuition said "no."

Oh, he's tried, dear man. The nervous twitch he acquired in the translation period between *Sanctus, Sanctus, Sanctus* and "Holy, Holy, Holy" now only appears when he notices *E Pluribus Unum* on a coin or stops in to the Quo Vadis Bar for a couple of glasses of Blue Nun.

His stuttering is still a problem, however — but you really can't expect a man to adapt overnight to the Kiss of Peace when his only public display of emotion in the last thirty years has been to hold his hand over his heart during the Pledge of Allegiance.

He's had his brief moments of open defiance, though. I'll never forget the second time he attended Mass when a movie screen and slide show replaced the homily. He was ready. I can see him yet — marching down the aisle, his collection basket filled with popcorn.

Women lectors brought on a rash; eucharistic min-

47

isters gave him a limp; and ever since Communion-in-the-hand, he wheezes from the Offertory through the Closing Prayer.

In the past few weeks it's been better — except for periodic nosebleeds if he happens to run across crouton-shaped altar breads. I really felt he was beginning to cope.

Until last night.

Our parish was holding its first liturgical dance class and when I came out in my green-for-joy body suit and my size 44 tutu, I thought he was going to have a stroke. I tried desperately to soothe him with that statement of reassurance that precedes every liturgical innovation: "But, dear, it'll only be done in good taste." (When he gagged, I knew we were in trouble.)

So, Peter, if you could only stop by the house for just a few minutes to give him moral support. But please, one favor: if you decide to come by chariot — bearded, sockless, sandled and wearing your toga — don't tell him you're a pope. That might just be the thing that would push him over the edge.

Concerned,

Lois

Mary Magdalene, *President*
Sinners Anonymous
Matthew, N.T.

28:8

Dear St. Mary Magdalene:

The fact that you "ran" to the apostles with your good news on Easter morning when you might simply have "gone" to them, or "walked," or at most, "hurried," prompted me to write. You see, "ran" indicates to me that you were possibly into the early-A.D. jogging scene and probably exercised to keep physically fit. I can see you now flipping through the Magdala Yellow Pages to find your neighborhood workout gym or health spa. I admire you for that disciplined obedience to the care-for-your body extension of the Fifth Commandment; but those of us who suffer from inoperative self-discipline beg for your non-judgmental understanding when it comes to exercise.

Personally, I would like to believe that anything even remotely resembling side bends, sit-ups, touch-your-toes or kick-your-legs is the work of the devil. However, my conscience doesn't always agree. During those brief and infrequent moments of doubt I do *try*. Once I tried running in place (in my place, of course: the public wasn't ready for a triple-X large sweatsuit or perspiration flashflooding). Within the first ten seconds I was so short of breath I anticipated an immediate and surely permanent out-of-body experience. I panted as if I were cramming for a last-stage breathing test like those given in a natural-childbirth class.

One other time I tried a spa. For years I had set up a mental block against the word *spa*. I kept insisting that it was a grammatical contraction — like "Where's Pa?" or " 's Pa comin' home for dinner?" I tell you, I found out in a hurry that the only contraction involved in a spa is muscular. Now, I've got muscles that haven't done an hour's work in 15 years, and I should have known that they would not come out of retirement without painful protest. I was so stiff and sore after my first encounter with "stretch and bend" that I had to take two-hour liniment baths every four hours.

Why did I make myself so miserable? Good question. Well, originally I had a choice — either self-imposed physical suffering of diet and exercise or a mentally deteriorating guilt complex inflicted by a society more tolerant of obscenity than obesity. Basically lazy, devoid of will power and incompatible with pain, I decided to go with guilt. I figured I could pass the buck and blame my pudginess on my kids. The way I see it, if I can be held responsible for every one of their major or minor abnormalities, the least they can do in return is shoulder the burden of my figure imperfections. (After all, it only amounts to about five or ten pounds apiece.)

You will note that I said "originally" I had a choice. That was before I won a month's free pass to this metropolitan fat farm. Now, the only thing stronger than my compulsion to eat is my obsessive delight

in getting something for nothing. I just *had* to take advantage of it.

I should have given up when they asked me to wear leotards. Me in a leotard is like a 25-pound tom turkey in a salami stocking. Reluctantly they settled for me in pup tent and bloomers. I went in through the back door after dark.

I hadn't been inside five minutes when my allergy started acting up. First the palsied shaking — then the swelling. It happens every time I come within ten feet of a scale. They weren't the least bit concerned about my discomfort; but they were kind enough to blindfold me before they checked my weight.

Following that I was ushered into the figure analyst. When it came to the description line reading "Bone Structure," she stared at me so long I got the impression she suspected I'd been inflated and that there weren't any bones there at all. For a moment I feared she might suggest exploratory surgery; but she merely shrugged her shoulders and filled in the answer space with a large question mark. It didn't help matters when I confessed to wearing two-size-small girdles — one for each thigh. After that she shook her head a lot. Her final analysis was that my right earlobe was in fairly satisfactory condition. The rest of me she stamped "critical."

Next I was put into a group of fellow "plumps." Immediately I decided that anyone under 150 pounds was a spy from some health-food store, to be avoided.

Our first stop was the carpeted and chandeliered torture room. I nearly fainted. You have never seen so much agony in motion — chrome fingers mercilessly kneading human flesh — vibrating poundage wherever you looked — grunts — groans — heavy breathing. I'd have fled in panic except that my instant friend, Size 48, was blocking the doorway.

With trepidation, I mounted a "going nowhere" bicycle and the attendant set the timer for two minutes. (She turned her back so I coasted for 118 seconds.) When they announced "sit-up time" I was certain I never would again. My heart was beating like a turned-on drummer in a rock group.

But the pool was delightful. There's nothing like buoyancy to "think thin."

The steam room was something else — a kind of group-therapy approach to offensive perspiration. The dry heat of the sauna made me a little delirious. I kept seeing my waistline (which disappeared after my first pregnancy and hasn't been seen since).

I probably would have been taken out by stretcher within the week, had not a kind and merciful fate come to my rescue. (The building was condemned for heretofore-unnoticed cracks in the foundation.)

I won't go on, and I'll also spare you the sordid details of my bicycling venture. (To this day my son's friends believe that his body bruises, sprained wrist, broken arm and swollen ankle were the result of a drag-race accident — I couldn't bring myself to reprimand him for not admitting that his mother ran into him on her bicycle.)

I guess, Mary Magdalene, what I'm really trying to say is that I hope it's true that only someone who has experienced the agony of exercise side-effects has the right to cast stones.

Lethargically,

Lois

Paul *(f.k.a. Saul)*
Consumer Affairs
   (Tentmakers Division)
Acts, N.T.

18:2-3

Dear St. Paul:

I read in our local diocesan paper recently that the Church, in its projected plans, will deal with consumerism. This is certainly an understandable decision in a time when consumerism is so "in" that somewhere, at this very moment, I'm sure a microphoned chrysanthemum root is making its statement on fertilizer effectiveness. However, the article failed to give an address for submission of consumer feedback, so I write to you. Since you have been a tradesman who undoubtedly dealt with tent consumers, I feel you are certainly qualified to accept, evaluate and disseminate the following observations from this consumer.

To be perfectly honest, I have never thought of myself as a church *consumer*. As a sheep of the flock perhaps, as a cell of the Mystical Body maybe, even as deteriorating muscle fiber in the sleeping-giant laity — never as a *consumer*. But, then again, I never thought of myself as a senior citizen until I overheard someone enumerating the advantages of "discounts for seniors."

So why not? CONSUMER I AM! If I can fill out parishioner census cards, parish council surveys and help-at-school sign-up sheets, I certainly can take the time to offer what hopefully will be some constructive consumer input.

Let's begin with the positive. I'm delighted with clocks, padded kneelers, wheelchair ramps, carpeting, drinking fountains, restrooms, dripless candles, air conditioning, words I can understand, about-face altars and hearing-aid confessionals. As a growing-up consumer, I was about as apt to see any of these in my church as I was to see anyone from my church in St. John's Presbyterian.

Unfortunately, there are also some negatives, which I feel compelled to present in a bit more detail. You see, while they are now no more than potential whispers of dissatisfaction, they might well erupt into shouts of revolt if church consumerism becomes some nit-picker's cause. And let's face it, the church will have a lot less trouble dealing with the complaint-department ramblings of someone like myself (who can't even make an authoritative impact on the fourth grade during a rainy-day classroom lunch period) than to meet head-on with some Madalyn Murray O'Hair think-alike.

Now, Paul, tent design, construction and durability might well have been the main targets of any consumer complaints you might have received, but I feel that church consumers might strike from many points. For instance, the reliability of some tradesmen hired for parish work. I must admit that it didn't reinforce my church-consumer confidence the day I glanced into the truck of the man installing our expensive new stained-glass windows and saw a complete set of super-size felt pens.

Then there are *vigil lights*. Truthfully, I'm just not getting the hourly flame mileage out of them that I have in the past, yet they haven't noticeably changed in size. Now, to a 20th century consumer who has seen candy bars shrink to the size of Band-Aids and watched bread loaves shrivel before my very eyes, this is highly suspicious.

Along the same line, I've heard rumors that a rather questionable group of beekeepers are peddling altar candles with less than the required beeswax percentage — and has anybody recently investigated (beyond labeling) the alcohol content of our altar wines? One just can't be too careful these days, what with the growing divinity status of the almighty buck.

Come to think of it, at the beginning of Lent a year ago I'm sure that the ashes crossed on my forehead after morning Mass had completely disappeared by lunchtime. This year I could still see a smudge or two at 3:15 P.M. You don't suppose someone along the way has been slipping in some artificial preservative?

Oh, and another thing: It might be advisable to do an occasional "number check." I have heard from a very reliable source in a neighborhood parish that B-15 and G-41 haven't been called once in their last five weeks of Bingo.

We should also alert our publicity chairpeople to consider the possibility of consumer complaints against FALSE ADVERTISING. Our Women's Club Bake Sale was advertised as "Straight from our Parish Ovens." One disgruntled customer pointed an accusing finger at my paper-plate contribution of Double-Stuff Oreos. (For the record, she'd have raised furor of another sort if I'd have brought my very own straight-from-the-oven cookie specialty — charred black-bottom oatmeal with cavity-cracking raisins.)

In the name of *energy conservation,* I honestly feel that the 150-watt interrogation bulb used in some confessionals is a bit much. It always makes me feel like I'm only one step away from a rubber hose or matchsticks under my fingernails. While I'm sure its purpose is to provide sufficient light to read posted prayers or Scripture readings, still I'd prefer something more conducive to an atmosphere of reconciliation and more energy-economical — like a 15-watt soft yellow.

Safety is a major concern, of course, so all parish folding chairs should have identifying labels — pincher, squeaker, wobbler, collapser. (While any of them could prove to be consumer-hazardous, I think the "collapser" would be the most dollars-and-cents disastrous should a consumer decide to sue for whiplash.)

Even the fire department could be drawn into a consumer uprising. Imagine, if you will, a Holy Saturday Vigil Service, a pew-filled church and each one in

59

attendance holding aloft a three-inch lighted candle.

Now focus in on one distraught mother trying to juggle a prayer sheet and her flaming candle in one hand while using the other to stop the circulation in the arm of her seven-year-old who is waving his candle high above his head as though he were a torchbearer for the Olympics.

In front of them sits a nervous grandmother whose built-in defense mechanism is hysteria. She is holding a dozing toddler who has nightmares about fire monsters.

Two pews behind stands a "hyper" teenage drama student who would consider an opportunity to scream "fire" as an improvisational triumph.

Complete the picture by placing a 200-pound usher with a heart condition in front of the most accessible exit.

An unlikely combination? Perhaps, but even two out of five would qualify any of our churches for the fire department's Disaster Potential Award of the month.

I don't know if the Church plans to defend consumerism at the assembly-line level, but I heard that some manufacturer has been approached with the idea of producing dashboard St. Christopher statues designed and advertised "For Your Wife, Sister or Girl Friend." The fact that the dear saint will be blindfolded and have his hands locked in prayer could well be considered sexist.

Which brings to mind discrimination. In all my years of browsing through religious-article stores, have I ever once seen a medal, statue or even holy card honoring St. Hortense? No! This void might well contribute to some poor child's insecurity. I realize it wouldn't be realistic to expect an image replica of every saint; but perhaps a number of nondescript male-and-female statues with fill-in name blanks across their bases could be made available. Who would know the difference? And the Church could chalk up Hortense Jones and Wolfgang Smith as satisfied consumers.

My husband just came by. He read over my shoulder and asked where in the original article I'd seen anything about CHURCH consumerism. Then he handed me my bifocals so I could see him scratch through my notes complaining about blurred print in the Missalettes, shook his head and left.

He may be right. I may have misunderstood the type of consumerism the Church has in mind; but it won't hurt to put this letter in the "Just-in-Case" file — just in case Ralph Nader should knock on some rectory door.

Observantly,

Lois

Tabitha *(a.k.a. Dorcas)*
Out-of-Body Experience Research
Acts, N.T.

9:36-40

Dear Tabitha (or Dorcas if you prefer):

I've started this letter at least a dozen times trying to find some diplomatic way to ask you a very personal question. Unfortunately I find that I have one style of diplomacy and that's "blunt," so here goes —

When you died and Peter, in response to your friends' urging, returned you to life — *did you really want to come back?*

Now I know your well-meaning friends missed you terribly, what with your recorded reputation of leading a life "marked by constant good deeds and acts of charity," but were *you* all that anxious to get back at it? (Please be honest because I promise I won't tell a soul.)

What prompts my question is the fact that it is already 4:15 P.M. — that I've spent all day standing in one line or another — that I have two meetings I should attend tonight — that I'm six weeks behind in my letter-writing — six years behind in my spring house-cleaning — that the checkbook does not balance — that I got a letter today from my sister-in-law to say that she, her seven kids, their pregnant German shepherd and their pet bat are coming to spend the summer —

that tomorrow I've got a dental appointment for a root canal — that my husband wants to join a couples jogging team — and that I haven't got a piece of chocolate in the house.

Just a few minutes ago I said to the dear Lord, I said: "O Lord, if a fatal cardiac arrest is scheduled for me anytime within the next six months, please make it NOW — this very minute. And please, Lord, if there are any roaming apostle-descendants in my vicinity with the powers of Peter, don't tell my friends."

Oh, I'm certainly not against living, Tabitha. There are lots of reasons why I might like to stick around. All my life I've been a militant proponent of heartbeat, brain-wave activity and all the loving that goes with them, but right now, standing here on catastrophe crest, I can see a few negatives. One in particular — and I'm sure it would be enough to convince me to want my "remains" to remain "remains" — is *cooking*!

The thought of no more cooking is absolutely euphoric — like clothes with no waistbands.

Do you know, Tabitha, that my mileaged hands have potato-peeler calluses, wooden-spoon splinters and panhandle grooves? That I've got burn scars from my fingertips to my elbows? That I have incurable taster's tongue, and that not a day goes by that I don't suffer from a touch of Fahrenheit fever?

In little ways I'm rebelling, though. I no longer

have the Thursday edition of the newspaper delivered, because that's when the food and recipe section appears. In our parish cookbook there's a blank page with my name at the bottom — one feeble outcry for apron retirement. I'm so tired of cooking hamburger that I've torn all the cow pictures out of my grandchildren's animal books. The only cooking timer I have in the house is the smoke alarm. I've even stooped to evangelizing a whole new culinary scare tactic — if it has to be boiled, fried, baked, broiled or even microwaved, it causes cancer. I don't like to shop for food, pay for food, cupboard food, refrigerate food, freeze food or cook food . . . eating it presents no problem.

Some laugh at the possibility that in the future we may be serving meals which consist entirely of capsules, pills and water. Let them laugh — for me it's a priority "pray-for." Of course, I'm not kidding myself, if I happen to be around when it becomes a reality, you can bet that some diehard Julia Child will come out with ten gourmet recipes for preparing water.

I keep hearing about those men whose hobby is cooking. All I can say is, if there's anything to this reincarnation thing and I get sent back human and female, you can be sure that my next husband-hunting qualification sheet will show "hobby: cooking" running a very close second to "millionaire."

It isn't that I *never* liked to cook. I used to teaspoon and half-cup it with the best of them. (Well, maybe not with the *best*. But I could whip together the basics in fairly palatable form.) At least there are no recorded cases of malnutrition among the kids. One or two may have had a little trouble with sugar-withdrawal when they left home and entered into the strange new world of nutritional "no-no's," but just because I *used* to like to cook doesn't mean I necessarily entered into a lifetime commitment. I used to like to jitterbug, but I didn't anticipate spending my social-security years hopping around in saddle shoes and bobby socks.

It's a shame Mother Nature couldn't have tossed cooking into the "that's-the-end-of-that" package deal that goes with menopause.

Oh, Tabitha, I suppose when the time comes I'll fight it all the way; but as of now, I just need your assurance that there's nothing wrong with wanting that wonderful feeling that must go with leaving behind forever "stir, simmer, shake and sauté." Ah, the marvelous world of yet-to-be.

Rest in peace (and enjoy it),

Lois

P.S. I just had this horrible thought — but no, a loving God wouldn't make me the only cook in a 24-hour purgatory diner.

III. AGE OF FAITH

(Golden Oldies from Canon and Calendar)

Cecilia, *Patroness*
Poets & Musicians Local 111
Feast Day
11-22

Dear St. Cecilia:

I wish I could write to you on a true *poetry* level, but I am definitely not in the iambic-pentameter Big 10. (You'll find me out with the Pop Warner crowd doing my moon-tune-soon-June thing.)

However, I feel certain that your Communion of Saints Manual on Patience and Understanding encourages you to deal compassionately with the less gifted, so here I am to ask a big favor.

On rare occasions I have an outbreak of rhyming which is always accompanied by the need to share. (An extension of my basic insecurity.) Needless to say, human-to-human friendships can only hold up under a certain amount of "listen to this" pressure. That's why I turn to you — asking for sort of a one-way pen-pal relationship between the Church Triumphant and the Church Militant.

I say "one-way" because I certainly don't expect you to write back. In fact, I don't really care what you do with any poemry I send you. (*Poemry* is just a word I made up to give my verse a little class.) I simply need the therapeutic release that comes with sharing, and I promise I won't burden you. I'll only send

68

something when I really need to relieve the pressure.

Attached is a five-line sample. I don't want to risk a saintly turn-off with anything lengthy.

> No, never will I have the chance
> To be part of liturgical dance:
>   I've a leotard pot
>   And graceful I'm not,
> So I'll "pew" while other folks "prance."

There, I feel better already. So, I ask again, please overlook a negative talent and see a positive need. (If my typewriter doesn't melt within two days, I'll know you've agreed.)

> I'm hoping
> while coping,
>
> *Lois*

P.S. So you will know that I'm not overstating the importance of verse-writers having a "sharer" outlet — I read in our local newspaper that a man held a cab driver at gunpoint and forced him to listen while he read some original verse. I don't want it to come to that. — L.D.

Paula, *Charter Member*
"Friends of Bible Experts"
Jerome Division
Rome, A.D.
347-404

Dear St. Paula:

I had this frightening premonition involving a friend of yours. But wait; let me go back to the beginning. . . .

Not too many years ago I was definitely a comfortable Catholic. I had the Mass, my rosary, St. Jude's Novena, my First Friday prayer book, the seven sacraments, commandments from both God and the Church, a bottle of Lourdes water and a mantilla straight from the Shrine of Our Lady of Guadalupe. I faithfully recorded every birth, baptism, First Communion, confirmation, marriage and death in the family Bible. Kept it well dusted and in plain sight. My crucifix, framed picture of Mary and plaque of the Last Supper all hung in appropriate rooms in the house. Statues of my favorite saints were conspicuously displayed.

My matches and vigil lights were ever ready for special intentions and my holy water was bottled and in the hall closet in case of thunderstorms, hurricane warnings, earthquake tremblings or burglar sounds. St. Christopher medals were mounted in the family car and crazy-glued to the underside of our son's bicy-

cle fender. A slightly weatherbeaten 18-inch plaster-of-
Paris statue of St. Francis stood among the weeds in
my back yard, patiently awaiting construction of his
grotto. I kept prayerfully in touch with heaven and
pretty much minded my own spiritual business — then
it started. (I should have known it was too good to
last.)

It all began with a small spin-off group from our
Altar and Rosary Society. They decided among them-
selves that they wanted to "go Bible."

Now don't misunderstand. I didn't mind that one
bit. In fact I commended them for wanting to read the
Bible, study it, enjoy it, draw great strength and consolation from it, even carry it openly wherever they
went, *but* it never occurred to me that they were going
to MEMORIZE it.

I think what got to me most was the feeling of
guilt. The more I heard my friends quoting chapter
and verse, the more I was forced to admit that about 99
and 44/100 percent of the time I hadn't the foggiest
idea what they were talking about.

Mine was kind of a Cecil B. DeMille-TV-special ac-
quaintance with the Bible. I was on pretty firm ground
with burning bushes, flooding waters, parting seas,
talking angels, scheming scribes and crowing cocks,
but that was it. My cast of familiar biblical characters
was little more than double the menu selection at a
popcorn stand.

The first time I heard someone mention Micah and Haggai I thought they were a summer replacement for Mork and Mindy. Oh, I did vaguely recognize the names Ruth and Sarah and Jacob and Aaron, but when I overheard someone talking about Zerah, Nahash, Joash and Mordecai, I thought some new foreign-born family had moved into the neighborhood.

With some reluctance I finally admitted (to myself, at least) that being envious or resentful or guilty was not the answer — half the parishioners, five out of our six nuns, both our priests and two weekend seminarians couldn't all be wrong. I pulled myself up by my bookmarks and went for "In the beginning. . . ."

The fact that I had only about a two-minute concentration span and retained all of three percent of what I read made me keenly aware that I would never reach the chapter-and-verse-quoting level. I did seek, however, to go beyond the "somewhere in the Bible I remember reading something about" plateau and was thrilled when after only a year and a half I could tell a psalm from a proverb.

I admit I've done a bit of bluffing along the way. Quite by accident I discovered the tiny 21-verse Book of Obadiah. (I would probably never have found it if that hadn't been the spot where I pressed the single sunflower my husband gave me on our 15th wedding anniversary.) Anyway, as soon as I discovered it, I knew that this tiny two-page book would undoubtedly be thumbed-past by most readers, so I immediately decided to use it as my inspired source of biblical knowledge. Within a month I had quoted more words from the Book of Obadiah than the poor man could have uttered in a lifetime. I tell you, Paula, in struggling to "belong" I paraphrased Scripture so destructively that, even now, every time I open the Bible, the pages curl.

My problem is, of course, that I'm faced with an insurmountable handicap — I can't memorize. My Baltimore repertoire consists of "God made me to know Him, love Him, serve Him in this life and to be happy with Him forever in the next." In secular circles I can come up with a brilliant "Dick. See Dick. See Dick run." And when it comes to *numbers* — forget it. (That's why I have engraved on the back of my I-Am-a-Catholic identification bracelet my phone number, my social security number and the combination to my junk-food safe.)

So this is where I found myself — struggling to overcome an apparent Bible block — when I had this horrible feeling that someone in charge of celestial immigration might issue an official statement that, after the first of next month, no one will get into heaven without first passing an entrance exam — and that said exam was now being prepared by St. Jerome. That's right, Paula, Jerome. Your *friend*, Jerome. The BIBLE EXPERT Jerome.

Well, we both know what kind of questions he'll ask, *unless,* of course, a friend of his — some woman friend, some woman friend who is a mother — reminds him of the scripturally handicapped and convinces him to insert a good number of basic Catholic-mother questions like:

> "How many twin-size sheets does it take to make three angel costumes for the Christmas pageant?"

or:

> "How many rosaries can you say between midnight and 2 A.M. the first night your 16-year-old is late getting home with the family car?"

Dear Paula, I truly hope that my premonition is no more than the warning of a guilty conscience, but if it isn't, please remember, an awful lot of us are counting on you.

Desperately,

Lois

Francis of Assisi, *Peace Advocate*
Animal Lovers, Inc.
Assisi, Italy

1182-1226

Dear St. Francis:

You don't know how hard it is for me to write this letter — hypocrite that I am. For so many years I have been asking for your help, using your beautiful prayer, *using you*, I suppose, because never, in all that time, have I told you — you the great lover of animals — that . . . that . . . that I DON'T LIKE DOGS.

I don't know why I haven't said anything except that it's just one of those things you don't openly admit — like finding fuzzy green oranges in the back of your refrigerator. Or, maybe it was fear of being ostracized by friends or hanged in effigy by the S.P.C.A.

It's crazy, of course, to worry about being branded as an outcast for not liking dogs in a country where it's become almost fashionable to "not like" *everything*. Even the traditionally American untouchables are under attack. In the past few years, look what protesters have done to the flag and celebrity daughters to motherhood. Apple pie, too, is high on the hit list of the anti-artificial-sugar activists. So why, just because I don't like dogs, should I cower in the closet corner long after the door has swung wide for others?

I must admit that I sense within me strong stir-

77

rings of revolt. I no longer feel the need for psychiatric treatment to see if, even subconsciously, I hate my wealthy aunt's Pekingese who inherited all her stocks and bonds while I sit here with her collection of souvenir pillows from every state east of the Mississippi.

True, I have searched my childhood, but I do not attribute my hostility to the fact that when I was seven a singing dog beat me out of fourth place in a local amateur talent show — although it does seem probable that my parents' decision to accept the package deal that enrolled me along with our German shepherd in obedience classes may have been a contributing factor. (Even now I occasionally get the urge to drop to all fours when I hear the word "heel.")

But whatever the cause, I have come a long way and can openly admit, at least to myself and now to you, that I just plain don't like dogs. Big ones, little ones, long-haired, short-haired, pedigreed or mutt. Even if they are wrapped in mink sweaters, sprayed with "Kennel Number Five," have their hair teased and ribboned, their nails manicured, or wear their very own hairpiece, it doesn't change things — they turn me off.

Some people don't like elephants; very few like skunks, and I have yet to know a hippopotamus-lover. So why should I be the heavy? Talk about discrimination!

Please believe me, I'm not soap-boxing, "Down

with dogs." They're fine — as long as they belong to someone else and stay away from me. And I'm certainly not kidding myself. The dogs, too, recognize an enemy behind the forced smile and manner of detachment I try to affect in their presence. Ours is definitely a mutual animosity — it takes two to be incompatible.

But give me credit, St. Francis. I've really tried. I figured that if kids could learn to like spinach, I could learn to like dogs.

First it was the dachshund who must have had some cross-breeding with termites in his ancestry because within days he had reduced my maple captain's chair to a three-legged conversation piece.

He was replaced by a cocker spaniel that brought with him his own, absolutely inseparable following of flea groupies.

I almost broke my leg when I tripped over a half-visible Chihuahua.

A Great Dane very nearly ate us onto the welfare rolls, and a pup of questionable extraction left me with half a pair of second-hand, rummage-sale Gucci boots.

It was then I signed a pact with my conscience: no spinach for the kids — no dogs for me.

If anyone else wants their lawns renovated, their glads transplanted or their flower beds fertilized, they can get a puppy. Me, I'll keep hoping for a gardener.

And another thing: I'm very self-conscious about being lapped, licked, sniffed at, growled at and slobbered on. When dogs pay me such personal attention I always feel that some article of clothing I'm wearing must have been made from a new synthetic blend of kitty litter, or that my cologne, a gift from my husband, must have been purchased at the same gag store where he got the fireplug whistle that only dogs can hear.

And, dear St. Francis, since I'm having this surge of honesty, I might as well go all the way. It isn't only dogs. To be perfectly frank, if I have any choice in the matter, the closest we'll ever come to having *any* furry pets in the house is that litter of dust balls upstairs under our bed.

One last thing, St. Francis: If this confession in any way makes you feel ill at ease dealing with me in the future, please let me know. I certainly will understand, and perhaps I can turn to St. Patrick — as I remember, he wasn't too crazy about snakes.

Relieved,

Anthony of Padua, *Intercessor*
Lost-and-Found Department
Padua, Italy

1195-1231

Dear St. Anthony:

Thank you so much for helping me find my car keys.

I couldn't imagine how they got into the refrigerator meat tray until I found the baby beef liver in the bottom of my purse.

Your job sure isn't easy.

With gratitude,

Lois

St. Cecilia *(follow-up)*

Dear Cecilia:

Hi again!

FANTASY ISLAND

Somewhere beyond the rainbow
   There's the answer to a prayer.
It's a Hershey chocolate island,
   And my friends will join me there.

Next to pools of melted butter
   We will live in French-bread huts,
And we'll pick from pasta bushes
   And munch on cashew nuts.

There'll be trees that bloom in pizza,
   And nearby we will hear
The babbling brooks of Gallo
   And the waterfalls of beer.

And whipped-cream clouds will settle
   Atop a shortcake mound,
And we'll eat and drink at leisure
   And never gain a pound.

It's all yours,

Lois

Thomas Aquinas, *Theologian*
"Big & Brilliant" Enterprises
Aquino, Italy
1225-1274

Dear St. Thomas:

I always knew that you were brilliant and saintly, but I was delighted to learn that you were fat — and, please, if it was a glandular disorder or metabolism imbalance, don't tell me. I need to believe that you simply overate. I also need to know something else — the name of a fat female saint, one to whom I can turn for help and encouragement. I have searched through biographical volumes and never once have I even seen as much as the word "plump" used to describe a she-saint. It's truly depressing, and I know — I just *know* — that up there among all the gals that have made it there must be at least one who left this world either in a Junior Plenty casket or was pleated, tucked and folded into a size regular. I don't care if she was hooked on Palestinian pastries, medieval munchies or was a contemporary chocoholic — I simply need a queen-size with a little influence.

In despair I had been holding out for the canonization of Pope John XXIII, figuring that he *might* understand since he was both pudgy and 20th century, but truthfully I can't imagine either of you roly-poly holy men "pigging out" over the weekend just because you hoped to diet on Monday — or donating every full-length mirror in the house (including the valuable antique in the solid oak frame) to the Harmonica-Lessons-for-Some-Deserving-Altar-Boy Garage Sale—or, for that matter, wearing a wig, dark glasses and carrying false identification when you went clothes shopping. I'm sure all of that would be as foreign to any man as pregnancy cravings. That's why I need a woman — a specific woman, St. Thomas. Having a "to whom it may concern" intercessor just doesn't fill the bill. I made up my mind to that the last time a priest assured me from the pulpit that "there are countless saints in heaven just like you." I wanted to stand up and shout, "NAME ONE!"

Believe me, I pray for strength against temptation. I know the power of prayer but feel mine hasn't been quite as effective since I've succumbed to the belief that I pray better after chocolate-chip cookies and milk. (My fat female saint would understand that.)

And it's not that I don't admire and envy all those lovely saints that I'm sure are slinking around some heavenly model agency, but let's face it, they probably had ALL their willpower bases covered. Not me — I'm a tower of strength when it comes to long-shot betting, hangover weekends and compulsive shoplifting, but one piece of apple pie à la mode can topple my tower. My spirit is weak and my flesh is weaker.

Really, St. Thomas, I'm not bucking for big-league sainthood (with a meditation span of about eight seconds, I know that I'm still sand-lot material) . . . and I don't expect to make the *Saints' Who's Who* via blood martyrdom (my threshold of pain being only slightly above hangnail, split ends or indigestion).

As for levitation, forget it — even if I were given such a possible indication of sainthood, I couldn't possibly perform under pressure. (As sure as the champions of my cause were watching, I'd stand there with lead feet and my beatification wouldn't get off the ground.) I must admit that for a time I hoped I might be in the apprentice stage of bilocation, since my body and my mind were so often in different places, but my doctor told me it was either vitamin deficiency or menopause. No, I'm just hoping to *squeeze* through the pearly gates with a little help from someone on the other side who remembers the false security of cherry-covered cheesecake.

Now, please, don't waste time searching for Saint Obese. I'll be happy with anything close to a five-foot-five, 38-33-44 lady with tapioca thighs and flabby upper arms.

(If you don't have any luck on your own, perhaps you could bring it up at the next Communion of Saints board meeting. I know she's up there someplace — maybe under one of those marshmallow clouds.)

Desperately,

Thomas More, *Lord Chancellor*
Twice Married — Once Beheaded
London, England
1478-1535

Dear St. Thomas:

I hope it does not embarrass you to have someone beg, because that's exactly what I'm going to do — BEG — complete with bended knee, folded hands and pleading voice: P-L-E-A-S-E, if you have any part in making policy decisions, don't let "couple confession" become mandatory.

I'm sure that at this point in time such a decision seems highly unlikely, but let's face it — if ten years ago I'd have written to you concerning Communion in the hand, someone reading over your halo would have snickered. This time I'm not taking any chances.

In case your antenna is not earth-turned and you think I'm kidding, let me assure you — I'M NOT!

The first time I saw a couple hand-in-hand it into the confessional, I happened to know that they were "whither thou goest, I go" honeymooners, and I figured that they were so oblivious to reality that they thought they'd gone through the door to the vestibule.

The next time, it was the husband-and-wife team that heads our parish council. I convinced myself that they weren't really going to confession — just holding

89

a brief executive summit meeting with the pastor in a location selected to avoid interruption.

But last night at our penance celebration I could deny it no longer. There, in the corner of the sanctuary set aside for confession, were the three of them — He-She-He. My eyes locked in shock position, and I wasn't able to blink for two whole minutes. I haven't been so paralyzed by disbelief since the second grade, when Sister Aloysius Perpetua caught her veil on the playground fence and I saw that she had hair.

It may well be that some married couples can withstand exposure to each other's pet peeves, gut feelings and temptations miscellaneous — our marriage has got all it can handle with mid-life crisis and tired blood.

Why ASK for trouble?

Just because Mrs. Carter was able to handle Jimmy's public confession of lust, don't expect the same from me. I don't want to hear my husband confess any possible "in his heart" reactions to the Dolly Parton look-alike who moved in next door. Can you imagine what that would do to my brittle-with-age self-confidence? What would I have to fall back on except escapism into self-imposed senility?

And in this new, casual, "even-if-it-isn't-a-sin, now's-a-good-time-to-get-it-off-your-chest" approach to confession, what if he says he wishes I'd lose 30 pounds? (With my willpower and self-discipline, the only way I could lose 30 pounds would be to start amputating.)

On the other hand, I'm certain he wouldn't want to hear me say his snoring drives me to the brink of arsenic in his morning oatmeal, because I know he couldn't stop snoring unless he plugged up every air passage in his body.

Unspoken compromise is to marriage what Scotch tape is to gift wrap.

I can't imagine that it would do either of us any therapeutic good if he knew that I kept $10 out of the grocery money to pay for the overtime parking ticket I got the day I stood in line an hour and a half to save 50 cents on four rolls of paper towels.

And why should *he* know that *I* know that the neighbor's dog didn't really chew up those glow-in-the-dark socks I bought him for his birthday. (I'm anxious to see what will happen to the matching shirt our daughter is giving him for Christmas.)

Enough about guilt — what about suspicion?

Don't you think, if I hear my husband confess that a good number of his sand-trap swings never show up on his golf scorecard, that I, being very human and very weak, would be somewhat suspicious the next time he keeps score at our weekly bridge game? Or, if he knew of my Alan Alda fantasies, don't you think he might view differently our shared enjoyment of

M*A*S*H reruns on our local television channels?

Come on, St. Thomas, as a married saint, you certainly MUST have a bit of "lie-a-little" experience to draw from. Complete trust in marriage, YES; but I'm sure that if God would have expected complete, whatever-you-think-say-it, absolute, unconditional honesty between married couples, He would have condoned either divorce or murder.

I tell you, St. Thomas, if "couple confession" ever becomes mandatory, there'll be a good many of us out searching back alleys for individual confessionals that promise encounter with the "go-in-peace" Trinity — penitent, priest and God.

Pleadingly,

Lois

St. Cecilia *(follow-up)*

Dear Cecilia:

Guess who?

RAMBLINGS FROM A FOLDING CHAIR
(which replaces a pew, in front
of which there used to be an altar rail)

They have postered each one of the stations
   In an effort to make them "today."
Cardboard and cut-outs and felt pen
   Are modernizing The Way.

The altar and walls are all bannered.
   The podium's streamered in green.
The crucifix hangs (I keep hoping)
   Behind the new portable screen.

My eyes are not downcast in reverence
   But because of this horrible feeling
That, should I look upwards toward heaven,
   I'd gaze on a crepe-papered ceiling.

'Bye for now,

Lois

Camillus de Lellis, *Patron*
Hospitals International
Lifespan, Italy

1550-1614

Dear St. Camillus:

On television today I heard someone refer to medicine as a religion; to the doctor as its high priest, and to the hospital as its temple in which to receive the sacraments of birth, healing or death.

I thought about it. I remembered the last time I visited the "temple," and I decided to share that "religious experience" with you — since I'm told you are the patron saint of hospitals.

To begin with, I'm convinced Mother Nature watches all those "look young forever" commercials and has demanded equal time. God has given it to her, and it's called Abdominal Surgery at the Half-Century Mark.

Now, you may be able to take a 50-year-old body, Clairol it, Max-Factor it, Arrid-Extra-Dry it, Playtex it, Cross-Your-Heart-Bra it, Leggs it, Dior it, expose it to nothing brighter than candlelight and pass it off for 48! BUT —

Take that same body. Remove everything that comes in a box; scrub off everything that comes in a bottle; tuck the Loving-Care highlights under a dis-

95

posable shower cap; stretch it out stark naked on a two-by-six-foot operating table under lights bright enough to illuminate the entire West Coast during a power failure, and you're seeing it like it is. (Fortunately, one kind soul with a weak stomach covered me with sheets.)

Ah, the irony of it all! My "high priest," with scalpel in hand, could have taken a meaningful step across the fat frontier. He could have removed 25 pounds of calorie accumulation, wrapped it in foil and sent it off to the Hershey Hall of Fame. But no. He took only a handful of malfunctioning memorabilia from my child-bearing days, and into the two-cubic-inch cavity he left behind, some overzealous beginner pumped 40 cubic feet of gas. Only then was I cross-stitched back together. It wasn't bad enough being gassed up at one end, but meantime at the other someone forced me to swallow the Mojave Desert. Bad breath was the only way to fight back.

Again in my room, I was able to muster up enough strength to lift one eyelid. I *had* to reassure myself that awakening to a mirrored ceiling was, thank goodness, only a sodium-pentathol nightmare.

One by one, scattered between my age spots, I discovered bruises in varying shades of black, blue, brown and yellow. Whatever feeling of femininity I had left was destroyed by three feet of outside plumbing taped to my leg and a nurse at my side measuring the contents of my very own plastic sewer.

Later, as I lay on my back looking down at the rumbling volcano of flesh stretching from hip to hip across my navel, there was certainly no consolation in knowing that somewhere beyond, in the Valley of Incision, lay yet a new line in my road map of varicose veins and stretch marks — my "bikini cut." It was almost ludicrous — giving me a bikini cut was like giving a hippo a dimple.

It took 48 hours, but finally I dragged myself to the scales and climbed aboard. After enemas, vomiting, pain and two days of nothing but liquid meals (which at the going rate were costing at least $20 each), I needed the one thing that might make it all worthwhile. I stared in disbelief. I had lost *one* pound . . . ONE LOUSY POUND!

I huffed and puffed myself back to my room, ripped open the lining of my suitcase, snatched out my Hershey bar and crawled back into bed.

No way was my temple visit a sacramental encounter. They can keep their medicine religion, their high priest, their temple. I've definitely not been given the "antiseptic faith" message, and any of their missionaries would be wasting time trying to get me to convert.

Amen!

Lois

IV. TODAY

(Pollster, Pontiff and Populace)

St. Gallup, *Director of Research*
Central Statistics Office
Heavenly Institute of Public Opinion

Dear St. Gallup (or whoever handles your opinion polls):

I know that I should never write a letter when I'm angry (which I am) because I may write from emotion rather than logic (which I will) and most likely I will regret tomorrow everything I write today (which is probably true), BUT — it's either this letter, a bottle of wine or throwing dishes. I've decided that it's not worth a hangover, and for sure we can't afford to replace dishes, sooo — I write asking you to take out your poll record sheet headed SHOULD PRIESTS HAVE WIVES? and chalk up an emphatic NO!

I hope your questionnaire allows plenty of space for "why," because here it comes:

At 9:45 this morning my water heater began to make noises as if it were possessed.

At 10:00 my "cold rinse cycle" filled with enough boiling water to shrink my favorite pure-wool cashmere sweater to a size 3.

At 10:15 the melon rinds, coffee grounds and eggshells that had just traveled through my garbage disposal came gurgling up around the clean dishes I had draining in the other side of my sink.

DEAR MOSES . . .

At 10:16 my plumber was responding to my hysterics with the assurance that I need not be concerned; that he would be at my house within the hour.

At 10:30 the melon-coffee-egg "surprise" went down my sink drain and came up in the toilet.

At 10:35 our son flushed the toilet.

At 10:40 the water was running all over the indoor-outdoor carpeting that it took me five years to convince my husband was practical in a bathroom.

At precisely that moment my plumber's answering service called to tell me that my plumber's wife had returned from Hawaii and he had gone to meet her at the airport, but not to worry — he would be over first thing in the morning.

As I listened, I watched Lake Bathroom overflow its banks and come streaming down the hallway. "By tomorrow morning I'll have my ark built!" I screamed, slammed down the receiver and began a frantic search for something I vaguely remembered my husband calling a shut-off valve.

What does my plumber picking his wife up at the airport have to do with priests not marrying? I'll tell you what it has to do with it!

Should an accident take me to the brink of judgment and a "serious matter with sufficient reflection and full consent of the will" have me earmarked for eternal damnation, you can bet your "Bless-me-Father" that I don't want to compete for a priest's attention with his wife, whose first-child labor pains are two minutes apart.

A bit dramatic? Well how about this?

I don't want to come to our pastor with plans for a lavish fashion show the day he told his wife she was spending too much money on clothes.

Or this?

I don't want to come seeking understanding because I feel overworked and find some priest's wife painting the outside trim on the second floor of the rectory while carrying a six-month old baby in a sling on her back, with homemade bread rising in the kitchen, and wearing a pair of coveralls she made by hand from four-by-five-inch denim pieces she bought at the church rummage sale.

And it's a cinch I don't want to waddle in pregnant with my ninth child and find that Father and his wife are either rhythm-compatible or graduated with honors from the Natural Family Planning classes.

Get the picture?

I know the above reasoning is selfish, narrow-minded, far from Christian and certainly immature, but that just proves my point. Some priests might marry women like me.

DEAR MOSES . . .

Oh, my gosh! My plumber just pulled up in front, and his wife is with him — and *she's* carrying the wrenches.

In haste,

Lois

John Paul II, *Pope*
Honorary World Traveler
Vatican City, Rome, Italy
1-9-8-4

Your Holiness:

I have been meaning to write to tell you that when I saw you get off your plane and kneel down to kiss the ground, I knew just what you were feeling. I did the same thing after my first (and only) plane ride. If the plane would have landed on a poison-ivy runway, or in the middle of the Sahara or atop an earthquake fault in action, I would still have gotten out and done the same.

I'm a terra-firma worshipper (within First Commandment limitations). For months after that trip I walked barefoot at every opportunity and carried a prescription bottle full of soil in my purse as a reminder of my blessings. Being a jet jockey aboard a metallic bucking bronco in that big rodeo in the sky is about as appealing to me as the prospect of major surgery without an anesthetic.

I will never forget that flight. I was TERRIFIED. But in time of such trauma I don't panic and I don't scream. I simply go rigor-mortis stiff, talk to myself and pray: "Please, Lord, take me UP!"

I felt that if my Creator was calling me to final judgment and was tuned in to my prayer frequency, He might grant me the option of crashing UP into the bottom of heaven rather than being strewn all over the earthen roof of hell. The expectation of being plucked intact from a cloud formation was much more pleasant than that of being gathered piece-by-piece and reassembled. (Post-Judgment transporation didn't worry me. I knew that once my eternal destination had been decided, I would get there sans air pockets, turbulence or mechanical difficulties.)

"You're being ridiculous," I told myself. "It's just your age." (Myself told me to look at the teenager across the aisle with the green face.)

I told myself that statistics show that air travel is one of the safest forms of transporation. (Myself said, "Put me down and I'll take my statistical chances.")

I told myself that this was an unusually rough flight and that . . . (myself told me to shut up).

I familiarized myself with all the exit locations and noted the people I would least like to trample.

I gritted my teeth to form a retainer wall against waves of digested food.

I was white-knuckled to my armpits.

Brow perspiration was splashing into the puddles already formed in my neck hollows. Nervous tension produced isometric contractions which would have been the envy of any body builder in the world.

I tried to recall my doctor's instructions on self-hypnosis for relaxation, but my mind was like his office on Wednesdays — empty.

The sins of my past life didn't flash before me in an agonizing instant — they dragged on like a 12-hour documentary.

I hated my husband for sending me on this vacation. ("There must be another woman.")

I hated the airline for putting me on this flight. (They didn't have to take their plane-hijacking spite out on me.)

I hated the Wright Brothers. (Just on general principles.)

My internal organs were so rearranged that I was certain I'd have to go to an oral surgeon for an appendectomy.

By this time every nerve end in my body was an antenna seeking heavenly acknowledgement of my S.O.S. — which is undoubtedly the reason I have no recollection of landing.

I do remember the pilot, co-pilot and ground crew unclinching my fists and removing me from the plane. I remember the concerned stewardess massaging back my blood circulation. I remember an airline representative assuring me that his company will provide speech therapy to cure my nervous stutter.

But most vividly I remember the ground-kissing ceremonies. Only when my trembling lips felt the solid security of asphalt was I absolutely sure that I had not been issued my celestial subpoena. At that grateful moment I dedicated myself to the less fortunate — to those who would fly again.

And I knew that most of them would fly again because it was faster — not because it was more fun. My task, then, was to take the fright out of flight.

After 37 minutes of regularly interrupted concentration, I had the solution — which solution I offered to the airline free of charge. I suggested that what they needed to attract the cowardly was a new dimension in air accommodations. Why not let the apprehensive passengers board through a special entrance where they would have a choice of sleeping pill, tranquilizer or injection. (Each could be given in dosages commensurate with the anticipated flight time.) "Revival upon arrival" would naturally be covered in the cost of the ticket. For those disappointed at not getting a peephole look at the scenery, "to and from" slides could be shown on a six-inch screen prior to departure.

These expenses would be easily offset by the low cost comparison between conventional seating and self-inflating stretchers. (In a plane built to carry 350 upright passengers, imagine the financial advantages of horizontal loading.) No meals would be necessary, although intravenous feeding could be available at a nominal extra charge. There would be no need for piped-in or screened-on entertainment since each pas-

DEAR MOSES . . .

senger could produce his own inner-cranium dream
spectacular.

The airlines did not jump at my unselfish offer, so I
am looking for an ambitious young pharmacist in-
terested in moonlighting, and we'll take over the
"composure concession" at all terminals. On a moment's notice, the printers will go ahead with our advertising posters — FLY THE FRIENDLY SKIES — TRAN-
QUILIZE! FROM HERE TO THERE WITHOUT A CARE.
HORIZONTAL — THE ONLY WAY TO FLY.

So, John Paul, hopefully we'll be in business by the
time you must take your next visit-the-flock flight.
Look for us.

Over and out,

Lois

POSTSCRIPT

Dear Reader:

Thank you for visiting my haphazard world. I hope you enjoyed your stay — and if you smiled even once, I'm delighted.

However, I do get shooting pains in my teenage-rejection scar tissue when I realize that you might not have smiled at all — that the only reason you've come this far in the book is because you are looking for a "satisfaction guaranteed or your money back" coupon. But don't worry, I can handle it. Always within easy reach is my super-sized aspirin bottle filled with tranquilizing M & M's.

Now I must say good-bye. I regret that we have not met personally but look forward to our doing so in the frown-free time of ever and ever. Please look for me. Undoubtedly I'll be the one with the "occupant" name tag, the square halo and the clipped wings.

With love,

Lois